CREATIVE CONFIDENT PAPER CO.

ONE LINE A DAY

FIVE-YEAR MEMORY BOOK

IN CASE OF LOSS, PLEASE RETURN TO:

_____

_____

_____

_____

SUBSCRIBE TO OUR EMAIL LIST
TO BE NOTIFIED OF NEW JOURNALS

GO TO URL AND SUBSCRIBE:

http://eepurl.com/gOiwlj

SCAN IMAGE WITH YOUR SMARTPHONE

HOW TO USE THIS BOOK

To begin, turn to today's calendar date, and fill in the year at the top of the page's first entry. Here, you can add your thoughts on the present day's events. On the next day, turn the page and fill in the date accordingly. Do likewise throughout the year. When the year has ended, start the next year in the second entry space on the page, and so on through the remaining years.

JANUARY 1

20 ⚫ _____
_____
_____
_____

20 ⚫ _____
_____
_____
_____

20 ⚫ _____
_____
_____
_____

20 ⚫ _____
_____
_____
_____

20 ⚫ _____
_____
_____
_____

JANUARY 2

20 _____ • _____

_____

_____

_____

20 _____ • _____

_____

_____

_____

20 _____ • _____

_____

_____

_____

20 _____ • _____

_____

_____

_____

20 _____ • _____

_____

_____

_____

JANUARY 3

20____●_____
_____
_____
_____

20____●_____
_____
_____
_____

20____●_____
_____
_____
_____

20____●_____
_____
_____
_____

20____●_____
_____
_____
_____

JANUARY 4

20 ___ •

20 ___ •

20 ___ •

20 ___ •

20 ___ •

JANUARY 5

20 ● _____

_____

_____

_____

20 ● _____

_____

_____

_____

20 ● _____

_____

_____

_____

20 ● _____

_____

_____

_____

20 ● _____

_____

_____

_____

JANUARY 6

20 ____ ● _____

_____

_____

_____

20 ____ ● _____

_____

_____

_____

20 ____ ● _____

_____

_____

_____

20 ____ ● _____

_____

_____

_____

20 ____ ● _____

_____

_____

_____

_____

JANUARY 7

20 _____ ● _____

20 _____ ● _____

20 _____ ● _____

20 _____ ● _____

20 _____ ● _____

JANUARY 8

20____ ● _____

_____

_____

_____

20____ ● _____

_____

_____

_____

20____ ● _____

_____

_____

_____

20____ ● _____

_____

_____

_____

20____ ● _____

_____

_____

_____

JANUARY 9

20____ ●_____
_____
_____
_____

20____ ●_____
_____
_____
_____

20____ ●_____
_____
_____
_____

20____ ●_____
_____
_____
_____

20____ ●_____
_____
_____
_____

20 ____ • _____

_____

_____

_____

20 ____ • _____

_____

_____

_____

20 ____ • _____

_____

_____

_____

20 ____ • _____

_____

_____

_____

20 ____ • _____

_____

_____

_____

JANUARY 11

20 ●

20 ●

20 ●

20 ●

20 ●

JANUARY 12

<u>20</u>　　●

<u>20</u>　　●

<u>20</u>　　●

<u>20</u>　　●

<u>20</u>　　●

JANUARY 13

20 ● _____

_____

_____

_____

20 ● _____

_____

_____

_____

20 ● _____

_____

_____

_____

20 ● _____

_____

_____

_____

20 ● _____

_____

_____

_____

JANUARY 14

20 _____ ● _____

_____

_____

_____

20 _____ ● _____

_____

_____

_____

20 _____ ● _____

_____

_____

_____

20 _____ ● _____

_____

_____

_____

20 _____ ● _____

_____

_____

_____

JANUARY 15

20 ● _____

20 ● _____

20 ● _____

20 ● _____

20 ● _____

JANUARY 16

20 ___ ● _____

_____

_____

_____

20 ___ ● _____

_____

_____

_____

20 ___ ● _____

_____

_____

_____

20 ___ ● _____

_____

_____

_____

20 ___ ● _____

_____

_____

_____

JANUARY 17

20 _____ ● _____

_____

_____

_____

20 _____ ● _____

_____

_____

_____

20 _____ ● _____

_____

_____

_____

20 _____ ● _____

_____

_____

_____

20 _____ ● _____

_____

_____

_____

_____

JANUARY 18

20 ● _____

_____

_____

_____

20 ● _____

_____

_____

_____

20 ● _____

_____

_____

_____

20 ● _____

_____

_____

_____

20 ● _____

_____

_____

_____

JANUARY 19

20 _____ ● _____

_____

_____

_____

20 _____ ● _____

_____

_____

_____

20 _____ ● _____

_____

_____

_____

20 _____ ● _____

_____

_____

_____

20 _____ ● _____

_____

_____

_____

JANUARY 20

<u>20</u>   ● _____

_____

_____

_____

<u>20</u>   ● _____

_____

_____

_____

<u>20</u>   ● _____

_____

_____

_____

<u>20</u>   ● _____

_____

_____

_____

<u>20</u>   ● _____

_____

_____

_____

_____

JANUARY 21

20 _____ ● _____

_____

_____

_____

20 _____ ● _____

_____

_____

_____

20 _____ ● _____

_____

_____

_____

20 _____ ● _____

_____

_____

_____

20 _____ ● _____

_____

_____

_____

JANUARY 22

20 ● _____

_____

_____

_____

20 ● _____

_____

_____

_____

20 ● _____

_____

_____

_____

20 ● _____

_____

_____

_____

20 ● _____

_____

_____

_____

JANUARY 23

20 _____ • _____
_____
_____
_____

20 _____ • _____
_____
_____
_____

20 _____ • _____
_____
_____
_____

20 _____ • _____
_____
_____
_____

20 _____ • _____
_____
_____
_____

JANUARY 24

20 _____ • _____

_____

_____

_____

20 _____ • _____

_____

_____

_____

20 _____ • _____

_____

_____

_____

20 _____ • _____

_____

_____

_____

20 _____ • _____

_____

_____

_____

JANUARY 25

20 _____ ● _____

_____

_____

_____

20 _____ ● _____

_____

_____

_____

20 _____ ● _____

_____

_____

_____

20 _____ ● _____

_____

_____

_____

20 _____ ● _____

_____

_____

_____

JANUARY 26

20 ___ •

20 ___ •

20 ___ •

20 ___ •

20 ___ •

JANUARY 27

20 ● _____

20 ● _____

20 ● _____

20 ● _____

20 ● _____

JANUARY 28

<u>20</u>　　● _____

_____

_____

_____

<u>20</u>　　● _____

_____

_____

_____

<u>20</u>　　● _____

_____

_____

_____

<u>20</u>　　● _____

_____

_____

_____

<u>20</u>　　● _____

_____

_____

_____

JANUARY 29

20 ● _____

20 ● _____

20 ● _____

20 ● _____

20 ● _____

20 ___ •

_____

20 ___ •

_____

20 ___ •

_____

20 ___ •

_____

20 ___ •

_____

JANUARY 31

20 ● _____

_____

_____

_____

20 ● _____

_____

_____

_____

20 ● _____

_____

_____

_____

20 ● _____

_____

_____

_____

20 ● _____

_____

_____

_____

FEBRUARY 1

20____ •_____

_____

_____

_____

20____ •_____

_____

_____

_____

20____ •_____

_____

_____

_____

20____ •_____

_____

_____

_____

20____ •_____

_____

_____

_____

FEBRUARY 2

20_____ ● _____

_____

_____

_____

20_____ ● _____

_____

_____

_____

20_____ ● _____

_____

_____

_____

20_____ ● _____

_____

_____

_____

20_____ ● _____

_____

_____

_____

FEBRUARY 3

20 _____ • _____

_____

_____

_____

20 _____ • _____

_____

_____

_____

20 _____ • _____

_____

_____

_____

20 _____ • _____

_____

_____

_____

20 _____ • _____

_____

_____

_____

FEBRUARY 4

20 _____ • _____

_____

_____

_____

20 _____ • _____

_____

_____

_____

20 _____ • _____

_____

_____

_____

20 _____ • _____

_____

_____

_____

20 _____ • _____

_____

_____

_____

FEBRUARY 5

20 •
_____

20 •
_____

20 •
_____

20 •
_____

20 •
_____

FEBRUARY 6

20 ___ ●

20 ___ ●

20 ___ ●

20 ___ ●

20 ___ ●

FEBRUARY 7

20____ •_____

_____

_____

_____

20____ •_____

_____

_____

_____

20____ •_____

_____

_____

_____

20____ •_____

_____

_____

_____

20____ •_____

_____

_____

_____

FEBRUARY 8

20 ___ •

_____

20 ___ •

_____

20 ___ •

_____

20 ___ •

_____

20 ___ •

_____

FEBRUARY 9

20 _____ ● _____

_____

_____

_____

20 _____ ● _____

_____

_____

_____

20 _____ ● _____

_____

_____

_____

20 _____ ● _____

_____

_____

_____

20 _____ ● _____

_____

_____

_____

FEBRUARY 10

20 ● _____

20 ● _____

20 ● _____

20 ● _____

20 ● _____

FEBRUARY 11

20 •

_____

20 •

_____

20 •

_____

20 •

_____

20 •

_____

FEBRUARY 12

20 _____ ● _____

_____

_____

_____

20 _____ ● _____

_____

_____

_____

20 _____ ● _____

_____

_____

_____

20 _____ ● _____

_____

_____

_____

20 _____ ● _____

_____

_____

_____

FEBRUARY 13

20 ___ • _____

_____

_____

_____

20 ___ • _____

_____

_____

_____

20 ___ • _____

_____

_____

_____

20 ___ • _____

_____

_____

_____

20 ___ • _____

_____

_____

_____

FEBRUARY 14

20 ● _____

_____

_____

_____

20 ● _____

_____

_____

_____

20 ● _____

_____

_____

_____

20 ● _____

_____

_____

_____

20 ● _____

_____

_____

_____

FEBRUARY 15

20 • _____
_____
_____
_____

20 • _____
_____
_____
_____

20 • _____
_____
_____
_____

20 • _____
_____
_____
_____

20 • _____
_____
_____
_____

FEBRUARY 16

20 ____ •

20 ____ •

20 ____ •

20 ____ •

20 ____ •

FEBRUARY 17

20 _____ ● _____

_____

_____

_____

20 _____ ● _____

_____

_____

_____

20 _____ ● _____

_____

_____

_____

20 _____ ● _____

_____

_____

_____

20 _____ ● _____

_____

_____

_____

_____

FEBRUARY 18

20 ___ ● _____

_____

_____

_____

20 ___ ● _____

_____

_____

_____

20 ___ ● _____

_____

_____

_____

20 ___ ● _____

_____

_____

_____

20 ___ ● _____

_____

_____

_____

FEBRUARY 19

20____ ●_____

_____

_____

_____

20____ ●_____

_____

_____

_____

20____ ●_____

_____

_____

_____

20____ ●_____

_____

_____

_____

20____ ●_____

_____

_____

_____

FEBRUARY 20

20 _____ ● _____

_____

_____

_____

20 _____ ● _____

_____

_____

_____

20 _____ ● _____

_____

_____

_____

20 _____ ● _____

_____

_____

_____

20 _____ ● _____

_____

_____

_____

FEBRUARY 21

20 _____ • _____

_____

_____

_____

20 _____ • _____

_____

_____

_____

20 _____ • _____

_____

_____

_____

20 _____ • _____

_____

_____

_____

20 _____ • _____

_____

_____

_____

FEBRUARY 22

20 ___ ● _____

20 ___ ● _____

20 ___ ● _____

20 ___ ● _____

20 ___ ● _____

FEBRUARY 23

20 _____ ● _____

_____

_____

_____

20 _____ ● _____

_____

_____

_____

20 _____ ● _____

_____

_____

_____

20 _____ ● _____

_____

_____

_____

20 _____ ● _____

_____

_____

_____

FEBRUARY 24

20 ● _____
_____
_____
_____

20 ● _____
_____
_____
_____

20 ● _____
_____
_____
_____

20 ● _____
_____
_____
_____

20 ● _____
_____
_____
_____

FEBRUARY 25

20 _____ • _____

_____

_____

_____

20 _____ • _____

_____

_____

_____

20 _____ • _____

_____

_____

_____

20 _____ • _____

_____

_____

_____

20 _____ • _____

_____

_____

_____

FEBRUARY 26

20 ___ ●

20 ___ ●

20 ___ ●

20 ___ ●

20 ___ ●

FEBRUARY 27

20 ___ ●

20 ___ ●

20 ___ ●

20 ___ ●

20 ___ ●

FEBRUARY 28

20 _____ ● _____

_____

_____

_____

20 _____ ● _____

_____

_____

_____

20 _____ ● _____

_____

_____

_____

20 _____ ● _____

_____

_____

_____

20 _____ ● _____

_____

_____

_____

FEBRUARY 29

20 ● _____

20 ● _____

20 ● _____

20 ● _____

20 ● _____

MARCH 1

20____ ●_____

_____

_____

_____

20____ ●_____

_____

_____

_____

20____ ●_____

_____

_____

_____

20____ ●_____

_____

_____

_____

20____ ●_____

_____

_____

_____

MARCH 2

20____ ●_____

_____

_____

_____

20____ ●_____

_____

_____

_____

20____ ●_____

_____

_____

_____

20____ ●_____

_____

_____

_____

20____ ●_____

_____

_____

_____

MARCH 3

20 ● _____

20 ● _____

20 ● _____

20 ● _____

20 ● _____

MARCH 4

20 _____ • _____

_____

_____

_____

20 _____ • _____

_____

_____

_____

20 _____ • _____

_____

_____

_____

20 _____ • _____

_____

_____

_____

20 _____ • _____

_____

_____

_____

MARCH 5

20 _____ ● _____

_____

_____

_____

20 _____ ● _____

_____

_____

_____

20 _____ ● _____

_____

_____

_____

20 _____ ● _____

_____

_____

_____

20 _____ ● _____

_____

_____

_____

MARCH 6

20____ ● _____

_____

_____

_____

20____ ● _____

_____

_____

_____

20____ ● _____

_____

_____

_____

20____ ● _____

_____

_____

_____

20____ ● _____

_____

_____

_____

MARCH 7

20 _____ ● _____

20 _____ ● _____

20 _____ ● _____

20 _____ ● _____

20 _____ ● _____

MARCH 8

20 ___ •

20 ___ •

20 ___ •

20 ___ •

20 ___ •

MARCH 9

20 ____ ● _____

20 ____ ● _____

20 ____ ● _____

20 ____ ● _____

20 ____ ● _____

MARCH 10

20 _____ • _____

_____

_____

_____

20 _____ • _____

_____

_____

_____

20 _____ • _____

_____

_____

_____

20 _____ • _____

_____

_____

_____

20 _____ • _____

_____

_____

_____

MARCH 11

20 ●

20 ●

20 ●

20 ●

20 ●

MARCH 12

20 _____ • _____

_____

_____

_____

20 _____ • _____

_____

_____

_____

20 _____ • _____

_____

_____

_____

20 _____ • _____

_____

_____

_____

20 _____ • _____

_____

_____

_____

MARCH 13

20 _____ ● _____

_____

_____

_____

20 _____ ● _____

_____

_____

_____

20 _____ ● _____

_____

_____

_____

20 _____ ● _____

_____

_____

_____

20 _____ ● _____

_____

_____

_____

MARCH 14

20 ___ ● _____

_____

_____

_____

20 ___ ● _____

_____

_____

_____

20 ___ ● _____

_____

_____

_____

20 ___ ● _____

_____

_____

_____

20 ___ ● _____

_____

_____

_____

MARCH 15

20 _____ ● _____

20 _____ ● _____

20 _____ ● _____

20 _____ ● _____

20 _____ ● _____

MARCH 16

<u>20</u>   ● _____

_____

_____

_____

<u>20</u>   ● _____

_____

_____

_____

<u>20</u>   ● _____

_____

_____

_____

<u>20</u>   ● _____

_____

_____

_____

<u>20</u>   ● _____

_____

_____

_____

MARCH 17

20 ___ ● _____

_____

_____

_____

20 ___ ● _____

_____

_____

_____

20 ___ ● _____

_____

_____

_____

20 ___ ● _____

_____

_____

_____

20 ___ ● _____

_____

_____

_____

MARCH 18

20 ● _____

_____

_____

_____

20 ● _____

_____

_____

_____

20 ● _____

_____

_____

_____

20 ● _____

_____

_____

_____

20 ● _____

_____

_____

_____

MARCH 19

20 ● _____

20 ● _____

20 ● _____

20 ● _____

20 ● _____

MARCH 20

20 ● _____

20 ● _____

20 ● _____

20 ● _____

20 ● _____

MARCH 21

20 _____ ● _____

_____

_____

_____

20 _____ ● _____

_____

_____

_____

20 _____ ● _____

_____

_____

_____

20 _____ ● _____

_____

_____

_____

20 _____ ● _____

_____

_____

_____

MARCH 22

20 _____ ● _____

_____

_____

_____

20 _____ ● _____

_____

_____

_____

20 _____ ● _____

_____

_____

_____

20 _____ ● _____

_____

_____

_____

20 _____ ● _____

_____

_____

_____

MARCH 23

20 ___ ● _____

_____

_____

_____

20 ___ ● _____

_____

_____

_____

20 ___ ● _____

_____

_____

_____

20 ___ ● _____

_____

_____

_____

20 ___ ● _____

_____

_____

_____

MARCH 24

20 ● _____

_____

_____

_____

20 ● _____

_____

_____

_____

20 ● _____

_____

_____

_____

20 ● _____

_____

_____

_____

20 ● _____

_____

_____

_____

MARCH 25

20 _____ ● _____

20 _____ ● _____

20 _____ ● _____

20 _____ ● _____

20 _____ ● _____

MARCH 26

20 _____ ● _____

_____

_____

_____

20 _____ ● _____

_____

_____

_____

20 _____ ● _____

_____

_____

_____

20 _____ ● _____

_____

_____

_____

20 _____ ● _____

_____

_____

_____

MARCH 27

20 _____ ● _____

_____

_____

_____

20 _____ ● _____

_____

_____

_____

20 _____ ● _____

_____

_____

_____

20 _____ ● _____

_____

_____

_____

20 _____ ● _____

_____

_____

_____

MARCH 28

20 _____ • _____

_____

_____

_____

20 _____ • _____

_____

_____

_____

20 _____ • _____

_____

_____

_____

20 _____ • _____

_____

_____

_____

20 _____ • _____

_____

_____

_____

MARCH 29

20 _____ ● _____

_____

_____

_____

20 _____ ● _____

_____

_____

_____

20 _____ ● _____

_____

_____

_____

20 _____ ● _____

_____

_____

_____

20 _____ ● _____

_____

_____

_____

MARCH 30

20 ● _____

_____

_____

_____

20 ● _____

_____

_____

_____

20 ● _____

_____

_____

_____

20 ● _____

_____

_____

_____

20 ● _____

_____

_____

_____

MARCH 31

20___ •_____

20___ •_____

20___ •_____

20___ •_____

20___ •_____

APRIL 1

20 ___ ●

20 ___ ●

20 ___ ●

20 ___ ●

20 ___ ●

APRIL 2

20 ●

20 ●

20 ●

20 ●

20 ●

APRIL 3

20 ●

20 ●

20 ●

20 ●

20 ●

20   ● _____

_____

_____

_____

20   ● _____

_____

_____

_____

20   ● _____

_____

_____

_____

20   ● _____

_____

_____

_____

20   ● _____

_____

_____

_____

APRIL 5

20 ● _____

20 ● _____

20 ● _____

20 ● _____

20 ● _____

APRIL 6

20____ •_____
_____
_____
_____

20____ •_____
_____
_____
_____

20____ •_____
_____
_____
_____

20____ •_____
_____
_____
_____

20____ •_____
_____
_____
_____

APRIL 7

20 ● _____

20 ● _____

20 ● _____

20 ● _____

20 ● _____

APRIL 8

20 _____ ● _____

_____

_____

_____

20 _____ ● _____

_____

_____

_____

20 _____ ● _____

_____

_____

_____

20 _____ ● _____

_____

_____

_____

20 _____ ● _____

_____

_____

_____

APRIL 9

20 _____ ● _____

_____

_____

_____

20 _____ ● _____

_____

_____

_____

20 _____ ● _____

_____

_____

_____

20 _____ ● _____

_____

_____

_____

20 _____ ● _____

_____

_____

_____

APRIL 10

20 ● _____

_____

_____

_____

20 ● _____

_____

_____

_____

20 ● _____

_____

_____

_____

20 ● _____

_____

_____

_____

20 ● _____

_____

_____

_____

APRIL 11

20 ___ •

20 ___ •

20 ___ •

20 ___ •

20 ___ •

APRIL 12

20 ___ ● _____

_____

_____

_____

20 ___ ● _____

_____

_____

_____

20 ___ ● _____

_____

_____

_____

20 ___ ● _____

_____

_____

_____

20 ___ ● _____

_____

_____

_____

APRIL 13

20 ___ ● _____

_____

_____

_____

20 ___ ● _____

_____

_____

_____

20 ___ ● _____

_____

_____

_____

20 ___ ● _____

_____

_____

_____

20 ___ ● _____

_____

_____

_____

APRIL 14

20 ● _____

20 ● _____

20 ● _____

20 ● _____

20 ● _____

APRIL 15

20 ___ •

20 ___ •

20 ___ •

20 ___ •

20 ___ •

APRIL 16

20 ___ •

20 ___ •

20 ___ •

20 ___ •

20 ___ •

APRIL 17

20 ___ •

20 ___ •

20 ___ •

20 ___ •

20 ___ •

APRIL 18

20 ___ •

20 ___ •

20 ___ •

20 ___ •

20 ___ •

APRIL 19

20 ● _____

20 ● _____

20 ● _____

20 ● _____

20 ● _____

APRIL 20

20 ● _____

20 ● _____

20 ● _____

20 ● _____

20 ● _____

APRIL 21

20 _____ ● _____

_____

_____

_____

20 _____ ● _____

_____

_____

_____

20 _____ ● _____

_____

_____

_____

20 _____ ● _____

_____

_____

_____

20 _____ ● _____

_____

_____

_____

APRIL 22

20 ●

_____

20 ●

_____

20 ●

_____

20 ●

_____

20 ●

APRIL 23

20 •

_____

20 •

_____

20 •

_____

20 •

_____

20 •

_____

APRIL 24

20 ● _____

_____

_____

_____

20 ● _____

_____

_____

_____

20 ● _____

_____

_____

_____

20 ● _____

_____

_____

_____

20 ● _____

_____

_____

_____

APRIL 25

20 ● _____

_____

_____

_____

20 ● _____

_____

_____

_____

20 ● _____

_____

_____

_____

20 ● _____

_____

_____

_____

20 ● _____

_____

_____

_____

APRIL 26

20 _____ ● _____

_____

_____

_____

20 _____ ● _____

_____

_____

_____

20 _____ ● _____

_____

_____

_____

20 _____ ● _____

_____

_____

_____

20 _____ ● _____

_____

_____

_____

APRIL 27

20 ●

_____

20 ●

_____

20 ●

_____

20 ●

_____

20 ●

_____

APRIL 28

20 _____ ● _____

20 _____ ● _____

20 _____ ● _____

20 _____ ● _____

20 _____ ● _____

APRIL 29

20 ● _____

20 ● _____

20 ● _____

20 ● _____

20 ● _____

APRIL 30

20 ___ ●

_____

_____

_____

_____

20 ___ ●

_____

_____

_____

_____

20 ___ ●

_____

_____

_____

_____

20 ___ ●

_____

_____

_____

_____

20 ___ ●

_____

_____

_____

_____

MAY 1

<u>20</u>　●＿＿＿＿＿＿＿＿＿＿＿＿＿＿＿＿＿＿＿

<u>20</u>　●＿＿＿＿＿＿＿＿＿＿＿＿＿＿＿＿＿＿＿

<u>20</u>　●＿＿＿＿＿＿＿＿＿＿＿＿＿＿＿＿＿＿＿

<u>20</u>　●＿＿＿＿＿＿＿＿＿＿＿＿＿＿＿＿＿＿＿

<u>20</u>　●＿＿＿＿＿＿＿＿＿＿＿＿＿＿＿＿＿＿＿

MAY 2

20 ● _____

20 ● _____

20 ● _____

20 ● _____

20 ● _____

MAY 3

<u>20</u>   •

<u>20</u>   •

<u>20</u>   •

<u>20</u>   •

<u>20</u>   •

MAY 4

<u>20</u>　　●

<u>20</u>　　●

<u>20</u>　　●

<u>20</u>　　●

<u>20</u>　　●

MAY 5

20____ •_____

20____ •_____

20____ •_____

20____ •_____

20____ •_____

MAY 6

20 ● _____

20 ● _____

20 ● _____

20 ● _____

20 ● _____

MAY 7

20 ● _____
_____
_____
_____

20 ● _____
_____
_____
_____

20 ● _____
_____
_____
_____

20 ● _____
_____
_____
_____

20 ● _____
_____
_____
_____

MAY 8

20 ___ • _____

20 ___ • _____

20 ___ • _____

20 ___ • _____

20 ___ • _____

MAY 9

20 _____ •

20 _____ •

20 _____ •

20 _____ •

20 _____ •

MAY 10

20 ● _____
_____
_____
_____

20 ● _____
_____
_____
_____

20 ● _____
_____
_____
_____

20 ● _____
_____
_____
_____

20 ● _____
_____
_____
_____

MAY 11

20 ___ • _____

_____

_____

_____

20 ___ • _____

_____

_____

_____

20 ___ • _____

_____

_____

_____

20 ___ • _____

_____

_____

_____

20 ___ • _____

_____

_____

_____

MAY 12

20 _____ ● _____

_____

_____

_____

20 _____ ● _____

_____

_____

_____

20 _____ ● _____

_____

_____

_____

20 _____ ● _____

_____

_____

_____

20 _____ ● _____

_____

_____

_____

MAY 13

20 ●

20 ●

20 ●

20 ●

20 ●

MAY 14

20 _____ ● _____

_____

_____

_____

20 _____ ● _____

_____

_____

_____

20 _____ ● _____

_____

_____

_____

20 _____ ● _____

_____

_____

_____

20 _____ ● _____

_____

_____

_____

MAY 15

20 _____ • _____

_____

_____

_____

20 _____ • _____

_____

_____

_____

20 _____ • _____

_____

_____

_____

20 _____ • _____

_____

_____

_____

20 _____ • _____

_____

_____

_____

_____

MAY 16

20   ● _____

_____

_____

_____

20   ● _____

_____

_____

_____

20   ● _____

_____

_____

_____

20   ● _____

_____

_____

_____

20   ● _____

_____

_____

_____

MAY 17

20   ● _____

_____

_____

_____

20   ● _____

_____

_____

_____

20   ● _____

_____

_____

_____

20   ● _____

_____

_____

_____

20   ● _____

_____

_____

_____

MAY 18

20 _____ ● _____

_____

_____

_____

20 _____ ● _____

_____

_____

_____

20 _____ ● _____

_____

_____

_____

20 _____ ● _____

_____

_____

_____

20 _____ ● _____

_____

_____

_____

MAY 19

20 ___ •

20 ___ •

20 ___ •

20 ___ •

20 ___ •

MAY 20

20 •

20 •

20 •

20 •

20 •

MAY 21

20 _____ • _____

20 _____ • _____

20 _____ • _____

20 _____ • _____

20 _____ • _____

MAY 22

20 ● _____

20 ● _____

20 ● _____

20 ● _____

20 ● _____

MAY 23

20 ● _____

20 ● _____

20 ● _____

20 ● _____

20 ● _____

MAY 24

20 _____ ● _____
_____
_____
_____

20 _____ ● _____
_____
_____
_____

20 _____ ● _____
_____
_____
_____

20 _____ ● _____
_____
_____
_____

20 _____ ● _____
_____
_____
_____

MAY 25

20 _____ • _____

_____

_____

_____

20 _____ • _____

_____

_____

_____

20 _____ • _____

_____

_____

_____

20 _____ • _____

_____

_____

_____

20 _____ • _____

_____

_____

_____

MAY 26

20 _____ ● _____

_____

_____

_____

20 _____ ● _____

_____

_____

_____

20 _____ ● _____

_____

_____

_____

20 _____ ● _____

_____

_____

_____

20 _____ ● _____

_____

_____

_____

MAY 27

20 _____ • _____

_____

_____

_____

20 _____ • _____

_____

_____

_____

20 _____ • _____

_____

_____

_____

20 _____ • _____

_____

_____

_____

20 _____ • _____

_____

_____

_____

MAY 28

20 ____ ● _____

_____

_____

_____

20 ____ ● _____

_____

_____

_____

20 ____ ● _____

_____

_____

_____

20 ____ ● _____

_____

_____

_____

20 ____ ● _____

_____

_____

_____

MAY 29

20____ • _____

20____ • _____

20____ • _____

20____ • _____

20____ • _____

MAY 30

20   ● _____

_____

_____

_____

20   ● _____

_____

_____

_____

20   ● _____

_____

_____

_____

20   ● _____

_____

_____

_____

20   ● _____

_____

_____

_____

MAY 31

20 ___ • _____

_____

_____

_____

20 ___ • _____

_____

_____

_____

20 ___ • _____

_____

_____

_____

20 ___ • _____

_____

_____

_____

20 ___ • _____

_____

_____

_____

JUNE 1

20 ● _____

20 ● _____

20 ● _____

20 ● _____

20 ● _____

JUNE 2

20 ____ • _____

_____

_____

_____

20 ____ • _____

_____

_____

_____

20 ____ • _____

_____

_____

_____

20 ____ • _____

_____

_____

_____

20 ____ • _____

_____

_____

_____

JUNE 3

20 _____ ● _____

20 _____ ● _____

20 _____ ● _____

20 _____ ● _____

20 _____ ● _____

JUNE 4

20 ____ • _____

_____

_____

_____

20 ____ • _____

_____

_____

_____

20 ____ • _____

_____

_____

_____

20 ____ • _____

_____

_____

_____

20 ____ • _____

_____

_____

_____

JUNE 5

20 ●
_____
_____
_____
_____

20 ●
_____
_____
_____
_____

20 ●
_____
_____
_____
_____

20 ●
_____
_____
_____
_____

20 ●
_____
_____
_____
_____

JUNE 6

20___ •_____

_____

_____

_____

20___ •_____

_____

_____

_____

20___ •_____

_____

_____

_____

20___ •_____

_____

_____

_____

20___ •_____

_____

_____

_____

JUNE 7

20 ●

20 ●

20 ●

20 ●

20 ●

JUNE 8

20 ____ ● _____

_____

_____

_____

20 ____ ● _____

_____

_____

_____

20 ____ ● _____

_____

_____

_____

20 ____ ● _____

_____

_____

_____

20 ____ ● _____

_____

_____

_____

JUNE 9

20 ____ ●
_____
_____
_____
_____

20 ____ ●
_____
_____
_____
_____

20 ____ ●
_____
_____
_____
_____

20 ____ ●
_____
_____
_____
_____

20 ____ ●
_____
_____
_____
_____

JUNE 10

20 ___ ● _____

_____

_____

_____

20 ___ ● _____

_____

_____

_____

20 ___ ● _____

_____

_____

_____

20 ___ ● _____

_____

_____

_____

20 ___ ● _____

_____

_____

_____

JUNE 11

20 _____ ● _____

_____

_____

_____

20 _____ ● _____

_____

_____

_____

20 _____ ● _____

_____

_____

_____

20 _____ ● _____

_____

_____

_____

20 _____ ● _____

_____

_____

_____

JUNE 12

20 ⬤ _____
_____
_____
_____

20 ⬤ _____
_____
_____
_____

20 ⬤ _____
_____
_____
_____

20 ⬤ _____
_____
_____
_____

20 ⬤ _____
_____
_____
_____

JUNE 13

20 ●

20 ●

20 ●

20 ●

20 ●

JUNE 14

20 ●

20 ●

20 ●

20 ●

20 ●

JUNE 15

20 ___ ● _____

_____

_____

_____

20 ___ ● _____

_____

_____

_____

20 ___ ● _____

_____

_____

_____

20 ___ ● _____

_____

_____

_____

20 ___ ● _____

_____

_____

_____

JUNE 16

20 _____ ● _____

_____

_____

_____

20 _____ ● _____

_____

_____

_____

20 _____ ● _____

_____

_____

_____

20 _____ ● _____

_____

_____

_____

20 _____ ● _____

_____

_____

_____

JUNE 17

20   ●

20   ●

20   ●

20   ●

20   ●

JUNE 18

20 ● _____

20 ● _____

20 ● _____

20 ● _____

20 ● _____

JUNE 19

20 _____ ● _____

_____

_____

_____

20 _____ ● _____

_____

_____

_____

20 _____ ● _____

_____

_____

_____

20 _____ ● _____

_____

_____

_____

20 _____ ● _____

_____

_____

_____

JUNE 20

20 _____ • _____

_____

_____

_____

20 _____ • _____

_____

_____

_____

20 _____ • _____

_____

_____

_____

20 _____ • _____

_____

_____

_____

20 _____ • _____

_____

_____

_____

JUNE 21

20   ● _____

20   ● _____

20   ● _____

20   ● _____

20   ● _____

JUNE 22

20 _____ • _____

_____

_____

_____

20 _____ • _____

_____

_____

_____

20 _____ • _____

_____

_____

_____

20 _____ • _____

_____

_____

_____

20 _____ • _____

_____

_____

_____

20   ●

_____

20   ●

_____

20   ●

_____

20   ●

_____

20   ●

_____

JUNE 24

20 ● _____

20 ● _____

20 ● _____

20 ● _____

20 ● _____

JUNE 25

20 ● _____

_____

_____

_____

20 ● _____

_____

_____

_____

20 ● _____

_____

_____

_____

20 ● _____

_____

_____

_____

20 ● _____

_____

_____

_____

JUNE 26

20 ● _____
_____
_____
_____

20 ● _____
_____
_____
_____

20 ● _____
_____
_____
_____

20 ● _____
_____
_____
_____

20 ● _____
_____
_____
_____

JUNE 27

20____ •_____

20____ •_____

20____ •_____

20____ •_____

20____ •_____

JUNE 28

20 _____ ● _____

_____

_____

_____

20 _____ ● _____

_____

_____

_____

20 _____ ● _____

_____

_____

_____

20 _____ ● _____

_____

_____

_____

20 _____ ● _____

_____

_____

_____

JUNE 29

20 ●

_____

20 ●

_____

20 ●

_____

20 ●

_____

20 ●

JUNE 30

20 ● _____

_____

_____

_____

20 ● _____

_____

_____

_____

20 ● _____

_____

_____

_____

20 ● _____

_____

_____

_____

20 ● _____

_____

_____

_____

JULY 1

20 •

20 •

20 •

20 •

20 •

JULY 2

20____ ●_____

_____

_____

_____

20____ ●_____

_____

_____

_____

20____ ●_____

_____

_____

_____

20____ ●_____

_____

_____

_____

20____ ●_____

_____

_____

_____

JULY 3

20 ___ ●

20 ___ ●

20 ___ ●

20 ___ ●

20 ___ ●

JULY 4

20 ● _____
_____
_____
_____

20 ● _____
_____
_____
_____

20 ● _____
_____
_____
_____

20 ● _____
_____
_____
_____

20 ● _____
_____
_____
_____

JULY 5

20 ●

20 ●

20 ●

20 ●

20 ●

JULY 6

20____ •_____

_____

_____

_____

20____ •_____

_____

_____

_____

20____ •_____

_____

_____

_____

20____ •_____

_____

_____

_____

20____ •_____

_____

_____

_____

JULY 7

20 ___ ● _____

_____

_____

_____

20 ___ ● _____

_____

_____

_____

20 ___ ● _____

_____

_____

_____

20 ___ ● _____

_____

_____

_____

20 ___ ● _____

_____

_____

_____

JULY 8

20 _____ ● _____
_____
_____
_____

20 _____ ● _____
_____
_____
_____

20 _____ ● _____
_____
_____
_____

20 _____ ● _____
_____
_____
_____

20 _____ ● _____
_____
_____
_____

JULY 9

20 ___ •

20 ___ •

20 ___ •

20 ___ •

20 ___ •

JULY 10

20 ____ • _____

_____

_____

_____

20 ____ • _____

_____

_____

_____

20 ____ • _____

_____

_____

_____

20 ____ • _____

_____

_____

_____

20 ____ • _____

_____

_____

_____

JULY 11

20 ● _____

20 ● _____

20 ● _____

20 ● _____

20 ● _____

JULY 12

20 ____ ● _____

_____

_____

_____

20 ____ ● _____

_____

_____

_____

20 ____ ● _____

_____

_____

_____

20 ____ ● _____

_____

_____

_____

20 ____ ● _____

_____

_____

_____

JULY 13

20   • _____

_____

_____

_____

20   • _____

_____

_____

_____

20   • _____

_____

_____

_____

20   • _____

_____

_____

_____

20   • _____

_____

_____

_____

JULY 14

20 ____ ● _____

_____

_____

_____

20 ____ ● _____

_____

_____

_____

20 ____ ● _____

_____

_____

_____

20 ____ ● _____

_____

_____

_____

20 ____ ● _____

_____

_____

_____

JULY 15

20   • _____

_____

_____

_____

20   • _____

_____

_____

_____

20   • _____

_____

_____

_____

20   • _____

_____

_____

_____

20   • _____

_____

_____

_____

JULY 16

20 ● _____
_____
_____
_____

20 ● _____
_____
_____
_____

20 ● _____
_____
_____
_____

20 ● _____
_____
_____
_____

20 ● _____
_____
_____
_____

JULY 17

20 _____ • _____

20 _____ • _____

20 _____ • _____

20 _____ • _____

20 _____ • _____

JULY 18

20 _____ • _____

_____

_____

_____

20 _____ • _____

_____

_____

_____

20 _____ • _____

_____

_____

_____

20 _____ • _____

_____

_____

_____

20 _____ • _____

_____

_____

_____

JULY 19

20 ● _____

20 ● _____

20 ● _____

20 ● _____

20 ● _____

JULY 20

20 ____ • _____

_____

_____

_____

20 ____ • _____

_____

_____

_____

20 ____ • _____

_____

_____

_____

20 ____ • _____

_____

_____

_____

20 ____ • _____

_____

_____

_____

JULY 21

20 _____ ● _____

_____

_____

_____

20 _____ ● _____

_____

_____

_____

20 _____ ● _____

_____

_____

_____

20 _____ ● _____

_____

_____

_____

20 _____ ● _____

_____

_____

_____

JULY 22

20   ●

_____

_____

_____

_____

20   ●

_____

_____

_____

_____

20   ●

_____

_____

_____

_____

20   ●

_____

_____

_____

_____

20   ●

_____

_____

_____

_____

JULY 23

20 _____ ● _____

_____

_____

_____

20 _____ ● _____

_____

_____

_____

20 _____ ● _____

_____

_____

_____

20 _____ ● _____

_____

_____

_____

20 _____ ● _____

_____

_____

_____

JULY 24

20 ● _____
_____
_____
_____

20 ● _____
_____
_____
_____

20 ● _____
_____
_____
_____

20 ● _____
_____
_____
_____

20 ● _____
_____
_____
_____

JULY 25

20 _____ • _____

_____

_____

_____

20 _____ • _____

_____

_____

_____

20 _____ • _____

_____

_____

_____

20 _____ • _____

_____

_____

_____

20 _____ • _____

_____

_____

_____

_____

JULY 26

20 ●

20 ●

20 ●

20 ●

20 ●

JULY 27

20___ • _____
_____
_____
_____

20___ • _____
_____
_____
_____

20___ • _____
_____
_____
_____

20___ • _____
_____
_____
_____

20___ • _____
_____
_____
_____

JULY 28

20 • _____
_____
_____
_____

20 • _____
_____
_____
_____

20 • _____
_____
_____
_____

20 • _____
_____
_____
_____

20 • _____
_____
_____
_____

JULY 29

20 ____ •

20 ____ •

20 ____ •

20 ____ •

20 ____ •

JULY 30

20   • _____

_____

_____

_____

20   • _____

_____

_____

_____

20   • _____

_____

_____

_____

20   • _____

_____

_____

_____

20   • _____

_____

_____

_____

JULY 31

20   ●

_____

20   ●

_____

20   ●

_____

20   ●

_____

20   ●

_____

AUGUST 1

20 _____ ● _____

_____

_____

_____

20 _____ ● _____

_____

_____

_____

20 _____ ● _____

_____

_____

_____

20 _____ ● _____

_____

_____

_____

20 _____ ● _____

_____

_____

_____

AUGUST 2

20 ___ ●

20 ___ ●

20 ___ ●

20 ___ ●

20 ___ ●

AUGUST 3

20 ● _____

_____

_____

_____

20 ● _____

_____

_____

_____

20 ● _____

_____

_____

_____

20 ● _____

_____

_____

_____

20 ● _____

_____

_____

_____

AUGUST 4

20 ● _____

20 ● _____

20 ● _____

20 ● _____

20 ● _____

AUGUST 5

20 _____ ●

20 _____ ●

20 _____ ●

20 _____ ●

20 _____ ●

AUGUST 6

20 ___ ● _____

_____

_____

_____

20 ___ ● _____

_____

_____

_____

20 ___ ● _____

_____

_____

_____

20 ___ ● _____

_____

_____

_____

20 ___ ● _____

_____

_____

_____

AUGUST 7

20 _____ ● _____

_____

_____

_____

20 _____ ● _____

_____

_____

_____

20 _____ ● _____

_____

_____

_____

20 _____ ● _____

_____

_____

_____

20 _____ ● _____

_____

_____

_____

AUGUST 8

20   ● _____

_____

_____

_____

20   ● _____

_____

_____

_____

20   ● _____

_____

_____

_____

20   ● _____

_____

_____

_____

20   ● _____

_____

_____

_____

_____

AUGUST 9

20 ● _____

20 ● _____

20 ● _____

20 ● _____

20 ● _____

AUGUST 10

20 ___ ● _____

_____

_____

_____

20 ___ ● _____

_____

_____

_____

20 ___ ● _____

_____

_____

_____

20 ___ ● _____

_____

_____

_____

20 ___ ● _____

_____

_____

_____

_____

AUGUST 11

20 ___ ●

20 ___ ●

20 ___ ●

20 ___ ●

20 ___ ●

AUGUST 12

20 ● _____

_____

_____

_____

20 ● _____

_____

_____

_____

20 ● _____

_____

_____

_____

20 ● _____

_____

_____

_____

20 ● _____

_____

_____

_____

AUGUST 13

20 ● _____

_____

_____

_____

20 ● _____

_____

_____

_____

20 ● _____

_____

_____

_____

20 ● _____

_____

_____

_____

20 ● _____

_____

_____

_____

AUGUST 14

20____ ●_____
_____
_____
_____

20____ ●_____
_____
_____
_____

20____ ●_____
_____
_____
_____

20____ ●_____
_____
_____
_____

20____ ●_____
_____
_____
_____

AUGUST 15

20 •
_____

_____

_____

_____

20 •
_____

_____

_____

_____

20 •
_____

_____

_____

_____

20 •
_____

_____

_____

_____

20 •
_____

_____

_____

_____

AUGUST 16

20   ● _____

_____

_____

_____

20   ● _____

_____

_____

_____

20   ● _____

_____

_____

_____

20   ● _____

_____

_____

_____

20   ● _____

_____

_____

_____

_____

AUGUST 17

20 •

20 •

20 •

20 •

20 •

AUGUST 18

20 _____ ● _____

_____

_____

_____

20 _____ ● _____

_____

_____

_____

20 _____ ● _____

_____

_____

_____

20 _____ ● _____

_____

_____

_____

20 _____ ● _____

_____

_____

_____

AUGUST 19

20 ● _____

20 ● _____

20 ● _____

20 ● _____

20 ● _____

AUGUST 20

<u>20</u>　●_____

_____

_____

_____

<u>20</u>　●_____

_____

_____

_____

<u>20</u>　●_____

_____

_____

_____

<u>20</u>　●_____

_____

_____

_____

<u>20</u>　●_____

_____

_____

_____

_____

AUGUST 21

20 ● _____
_____
_____
_____

20 ● _____
_____
_____
_____

20 ● _____
_____
_____
_____

20 ● _____
_____
_____
_____

20 ● _____
_____
_____
_____

AUGUST 22

20 _____ ● _____

_____

_____

_____

20 _____ ● _____

_____

_____

_____

20 _____ ● _____

_____

_____

_____

20 _____ ● _____

_____

_____

_____

20 _____ ● _____

_____

_____

_____

AUGUST 23

20 _____ ● _____

_____

_____

_____

20 _____ ● _____

_____

_____

_____

20 _____ ● _____

_____

_____

_____

20 _____ ● _____

_____

_____

_____

20 _____ ● _____

_____

_____

_____

AUGUST 24

20 • _____

_____

_____

_____

20 • _____

_____

_____

_____

20 • _____

_____

_____

_____

20 • _____

_____

_____

_____

20 • _____

_____

_____

_____

20   ● _____

_____

_____

_____

20   ● _____

_____

_____

_____

20   ● _____

_____

_____

_____

20   ● _____

_____

_____

_____

20   ● _____

_____

_____

_____

AUGUST 26

20 _____ ● _____

_____

_____

_____

20 _____ ● _____

_____

_____

_____

20 _____ ● _____

_____

_____

_____

20 _____ ● _____

_____

_____

_____

20 _____ ● _____

_____

_____

_____

AUGUST 27

20 •
_____

20 •
_____

20 •
_____

20 •
_____

20 •
_____

AUGUST 28

20 ____ ● _____

_____

_____

_____

20 ____ ● _____

_____

_____

_____

20 ____ ● _____

_____

_____

_____

20 ____ ● _____

_____

_____

_____

20 ____ ● _____

_____

_____

_____

AUGUST 29

20 ● _____

_____

_____

_____

20 ● _____

_____

_____

_____

20 ● _____

_____

_____

_____

20 ● _____

_____

_____

_____

20 ● _____

_____

_____

_____

AUGUST 30

20 ● _____

_____

_____

_____

20 ● _____

_____

_____

_____

20 ● _____

_____

_____

_____

20 ● _____

_____

_____

_____

20 ● _____

_____

_____

_____

AUGUST 31

20 _____ • _____

_____

_____

_____

20 _____ • _____

_____

_____

_____

20 _____ • _____

_____

_____

_____

20 _____ • _____

_____

_____

_____

20 _____ • _____

_____

_____

_____

SEPTEMBER 1

20 ● _____
_____
_____
_____

20 ● _____
_____
_____
_____

20 ● _____
_____
_____
_____

20 ● _____
_____
_____
_____

20 ● _____
_____
_____
_____

SEPTEMBER 2

20_____ •_____
_____
_____
_____

20_____ •_____
_____
_____
_____

20_____ •_____
_____
_____
_____

20_____ •_____
_____
_____
_____

20_____ •_____
_____
_____
_____

SEPTEMBER 3

20____ ● _____

_____

_____

_____

20____ ● _____

_____

_____

_____

20____ ● _____

_____

_____

_____

20____ ● _____

_____

_____

_____

20____ ● _____

_____

_____

_____

SEPTEMBER 4

20 •

20 •

20 •

20 •

20 •

SEPTEMBER 5

20   • _____

_____

_____

_____

20   • _____

_____

_____

_____

20   • _____

_____

_____

_____

20   • _____

_____

_____

_____

20   • _____

_____

_____

_____

SEPTEMBER 6

20 • _____

_____

_____

_____

20 • _____

_____

_____

_____

20 • _____

_____

_____

_____

20 • _____

_____

_____

_____

20 • _____

_____

_____

_____

SEPTEMBER 7

20 ____ • _____

_____

_____

_____

20 ____ • _____

_____

_____

_____

20 ____ • _____

_____

_____

_____

20 ____ • _____

_____

_____

_____

20 ____ • _____

_____

_____

_____

SEPTEMBER 8

20 •

20 •

20 •

20 •

20 •

SEPTEMBER 9

20   ●

_____

20   ●

_____

20   ●

_____

20   ●

_____

20   ●

_____

SEPTEMBER 10

20   ●

_____

_____

_____

_____

20   ●

_____

_____

_____

20   ●

_____

_____

_____

20   ●

_____

_____

_____

20   ●

_____

_____

_____

SEPTEMBER 11

20 _____ • _____

20 _____ • _____

20 _____ • _____

20 _____ • _____

20 _____ • _____

SEPTEMBER 12

20 ● _____

20 ● _____

20 ● _____

20 ● _____

20 ● _____

SEPTEMBER 13

20 ● _____
_____
_____
_____

20 ● _____
_____
_____
_____

20 ● _____
_____
_____
_____

20 ● _____
_____
_____
_____

20 ● _____
_____
_____
_____

SEPTEMBER 14

20 _____ ●

20 _____ ●

20 _____ ●

20 _____ ●

20 _____ ●

SEPTEMBER 15

20 ● _____
_____
_____
_____

20 ● _____
_____
_____
_____

20 ● _____
_____
_____
_____

20 ● _____
_____
_____
_____

20 ● _____
_____
_____
_____

SEPTEMBER 16

20 ___ •

20 ___ •

20 ___ •

20 ___ •

20 ___ •

SEPTEMBER 17

20 ___ ● _____

_____

_____

_____

20 ___ ● _____

_____

_____

_____

20 ___ ● _____

_____

_____

_____

20 ___ ● _____

_____

_____

_____

20 ___ ● _____

_____

_____

_____

_____

SEPTEMBER 18

20 ● _____

_____

_____

_____

20 ● _____

_____

_____

_____

20 ● _____

_____

_____

_____

20 ● _____

_____

_____

_____

20 ● _____

_____

_____

_____

SEPTEMBER 19

20 ● _____
_____
_____
_____

20 ● _____
_____
_____
_____

20 ● _____
_____
_____
_____

20 ● _____
_____
_____
_____

20 ● _____
_____
_____
_____

20 _____ ● _____

_____

_____

_____

20 _____ ● _____

_____

_____

_____

20 _____ ● _____

_____

_____

_____

20 _____ ● _____

_____

_____

_____

20 _____ ● _____

_____

_____

_____

SEPTEMBER 21

20 _____ ● _____

_____

_____

_____

20 _____ ● _____

_____

_____

_____

20 _____ ● _____

_____

_____

_____

20 _____ ● _____

_____

_____

_____

20 _____ ● _____

_____

_____

_____

SEPTEMBER 22

20 _____ • _____

_____

_____

_____

20 _____ • _____

_____

_____

_____

20 _____ • _____

_____

_____

_____

20 _____ • _____

_____

_____

_____

20 _____ • _____

_____

_____

_____

SEPTEMBER 23

20   •
_____

_____

_____

_____

20   •
_____

_____

_____

_____

20   •
_____

_____

_____

_____

20   •
_____

_____

_____

_____

20   •
_____

_____

_____

_____

SEPTEMBER 24

20 _____ ● _____

_____

_____

_____

20 _____ ● _____

_____

_____

_____

20 _____ ● _____

_____

_____

_____

20 _____ ● _____

_____

_____

_____

20 _____ ● _____

_____

_____

_____

SEPTEMBER 25

20 _____ • _____

_____

_____

_____

20 _____ • _____

_____

_____

_____

20 _____ • _____

_____

_____

_____

20 _____ • _____

_____

_____

_____

20 _____ • _____

_____

_____

_____

_____

SEPTEMBER 26

20 _____ ● _____

_____

_____

_____

20 _____ ● _____

_____

_____

_____

20 _____ ● _____

_____

_____

_____

20 _____ ● _____

_____

_____

_____

20 _____ ● _____

_____

_____

_____

SEPTEMBER 27

20 _____ ● _____

_____

_____

_____

20 _____ ● _____

_____

_____

_____

20 _____ ● _____

_____

_____

_____

20 _____ ● _____

_____

_____

_____

20 _____ ● _____

_____

_____

_____

SEPTEMBER 28

20 _____ • _____

_____

_____

_____

20 _____ • _____

_____

_____

_____

20 _____ • _____

_____

_____

_____

20 _____ • _____

_____

_____

_____

20 _____ • _____

_____

_____

_____

SEPTEMBER 29

20 •

_____

20 •

_____

20 •

_____

20 •

_____

20 •

_____

SEPTEMBER 30

20 _____ • _____

_____

_____

_____

20 _____ • _____

_____

_____

_____

20 _____ • _____

_____

_____

_____

20 _____ • _____

_____

_____

_____

20 _____ • _____

_____

_____

_____

OCTOBER 1

20 ● _____

20 ● _____

20 ● _____

20 ● _____

20 ● _____

OCTOBER 2

20 _____ • _____

_____

_____

_____

20 _____ • _____

_____

_____

_____

20 _____ • _____

_____

_____

_____

20 _____ • _____

_____

_____

_____

20 _____ • _____

_____

_____

_____

OCTOBER 3

20 ● _____

_____

_____

_____

20 ● _____

_____

_____

_____

20 ● _____

_____

_____

_____

20 ● _____

_____

_____

_____

20 ● _____

_____

_____

_____

OCTOBER 4

20 ___ • _____
_____
_____
_____

20 ___ • _____
_____
_____
_____

20 ___ • _____
_____
_____
_____

20 ___ • _____
_____
_____
_____

20 ___ • _____
_____
_____
_____

OCTOBER 5

20 ● _____

_____

_____

_____

20 ● _____

_____

_____

_____

20 ● _____

_____

_____

_____

20 ● _____

_____

_____

_____

20 ● _____

_____

_____

_____

OCTOBER 6

20 ● _____
_____
_____
_____

20 ● _____
_____
_____
_____

20 ● _____
_____
_____
_____

20 ● _____
_____
_____
_____

20 ● _____
_____
_____
_____

OCTOBER 7

20___ • _____
_____
_____
_____

20___ • _____
_____
_____
_____

20___ • _____
_____
_____
_____

20___ • _____
_____
_____
_____

20___ • _____
_____
_____
_____

OCTOBER 8

20 •

_____

20 •

_____

20 •

_____

20 •

_____

20 •

_____

OCTOBER 9

20 ● _____

_____

_____

_____

20 ● _____

_____

_____

_____

20 ● _____

_____

_____

_____

20 ● _____

_____

_____

_____

20 ● _____

_____

_____

_____

_____

OCTOBER 10

20 _____ ● _____

_____

_____

_____

20 _____ ● _____

_____

_____

_____

20 _____ ● _____

_____

_____

_____

20 _____ ● _____

_____

_____

_____

20 _____ ● _____

_____

_____

_____

OCTOBER 11

20 • _____
_____
_____
_____

20 • _____
_____
_____
_____

20 • _____
_____
_____
_____

20 • _____
_____
_____
_____

20 • _____
_____
_____
_____

OCTOBER 12

20 _____ ● _____

_____

_____

_____

20 _____ ● _____

_____

_____

_____

20 _____ ● _____

_____

_____

_____

20 _____ ● _____

_____

_____

_____

20 _____ ● _____

_____

_____

_____

OCTOBER 13

20 _____ ● _____

_____

_____

_____

20 _____ ● _____

_____

_____

_____

20 _____ ● _____

_____

_____

_____

20 _____ ● _____

_____

_____

_____

20 _____ ● _____

_____

_____

_____

OCTOBER 14

20 •

_____

20 •

_____

20 •

_____

20 •

_____

20 •

_____

OCTOBER 15

20 _____ ● _____

_____

_____

_____

20 _____ ● _____

_____

_____

_____

20 _____ ● _____

_____

_____

_____

20 _____ ● _____

_____

_____

_____

20 _____ ● _____

_____

_____

_____

OCTOBER 16

20 ● _____

20 ● _____

20 ● _____

20 ● _____

20 ● _____

OCTOBER 17

<u>20</u>　●　_____
_____
_____
_____

<u>20</u>　●　_____
_____
_____
_____

<u>20</u>　●　_____
_____
_____
_____

<u>20</u>　●　_____
_____
_____
_____

<u>20</u>　●　_____
_____
_____
_____

OCTOBER 18

20 _____ ● _____
_____
_____
_____

20 _____ ● _____
_____
_____
_____

20 _____ ● _____
_____
_____
_____

20 _____ ● _____
_____
_____
_____

20 _____ ● _____
_____
_____
_____

OCTOBER 19

20 •

_____

20 •

_____

20 •

_____

20 •

_____

20 •

_____

OCTOBER 20

20 ● _____

_____

_____

_____

20 ● _____

_____

_____

_____

20 ● _____

_____

_____

_____

20 ● _____

_____

_____

_____

20 ● _____

_____

_____

_____

OCTOBER 21

20 _____ ● _____

_____

_____

_____

20 _____ ● _____

_____

_____

_____

20 _____ ● _____

_____

_____

_____

20 _____ ● _____

_____

_____

_____

20 _____ ● _____

_____

_____

_____

OCTOBER 22

20 _____ • _____

_____

_____

_____

20 _____ • _____

_____

_____

_____

20 _____ • _____

_____

_____

_____

20 _____ • _____

_____

_____

_____

20 _____ • _____

_____

_____

_____

OCTOBER 23

20 ● _____

20 ● _____

20 ● _____

20 ● _____

20 ● _____

OCTOBER 24

20 _____ • _____

_____

_____

_____

20 _____ • _____

_____

_____

_____

20 _____ • _____

_____

_____

_____

20 _____ • _____

_____

_____

_____

20 _____ • _____

_____

_____

_____

OCTOBER 25

20 _____ ● _____

_____

_____

_____

20 _____ ● _____

_____

_____

_____

20 _____ ● _____

_____

_____

_____

20 _____ ● _____

_____

_____

_____

20 _____ ● _____

_____

_____

_____

OCTOBER 26

20 _____ • _____

_____

_____

_____

20 _____ • _____

_____

_____

_____

20 _____ • _____

_____

_____

_____

20 _____ • _____

_____

_____

_____

20 _____ • _____

_____

_____

_____

OCTOBER 27

20 _____ ● _____

_____

_____

_____

20 _____ ● _____

_____

_____

_____

20 _____ ● _____

_____

_____

_____

20 _____ ● _____

_____

_____

_____

20 _____ ● _____

_____

_____

_____

OCTOBER 28

20 ● _____

_____

_____

_____

20 ● _____

_____

_____

_____

20 ● _____

_____

_____

_____

20 ● _____

_____

_____

_____

20 ● _____

_____

_____

_____

OCTOBER 29

20 ____ ● _____

_____

_____

_____

20 ____ ● _____

_____

_____

_____

20 ____ ● _____

_____

_____

_____

20 ____ ● _____

_____

_____

_____

20 ____ ● _____

_____

_____

_____

OCTOBER 30

20 _____ • _____

_____

_____

_____

20 _____ • _____

_____

_____

_____

20 _____ • _____

_____

_____

_____

20 _____ • _____

_____

_____

_____

20 _____ • _____

_____

_____

_____

OCTOBER 31

20 _____ ● _____

_____

_____

_____

20 _____ ● _____

_____

_____

_____

20 _____ ● _____

_____

_____

_____

20 _____ ● _____

_____

_____

_____

20 _____ ● _____

_____

_____

_____

NOVEMBER 1

20 ● _____

_____

_____

_____

20 ● _____

_____

_____

_____

20 ● _____

_____

_____

_____

20 ● _____

_____

_____

_____

20 ● _____

_____

_____

_____

NOVEMBER 2

20 • _____

_____

_____

_____

20 • _____

_____

_____

_____

20 • _____

_____

_____

_____

20 • _____

_____

_____

_____

20 • _____

_____

_____

_____

NOVEMBER 3

20 _____ ● _____

_____

_____

_____

20 _____ ● _____

_____

_____

_____

20 _____ ● _____

_____

_____

_____

20 _____ ● _____

_____

_____

_____

20 _____ ● _____

_____

_____

_____

NOVEMBER 4

20___ ●_____

_____

_____

_____

20___ ●_____

_____

_____

_____

20___ ●_____

_____

_____

_____

20___ ●_____

_____

_____

_____

20___ ●_____

_____

_____

_____

NOVEMBER 5

20 ● _____
_____
_____
_____

20 ● _____
_____
_____
_____

20 ● _____
_____
_____
_____

20 ● _____
_____
_____
_____

20 ● _____
_____
_____
_____

NOVEMBER 6

20 ● _____

_____

_____

_____

20 ● _____

_____

_____

_____

20 ● _____

_____

_____

_____

20 ● _____

_____

_____

_____

20 ● _____

_____

_____

_____

NOVEMBER 7

20 _____ • _____

_____

_____

_____

20 _____ • _____

_____

_____

_____

20 _____ • _____

_____

_____

_____

20 _____ • _____

_____

_____

_____

20 _____ • _____

_____

_____

_____

NOVEMBER 8

20 _____ ● _____

_____

_____

_____

20 _____ ● _____

_____

_____

_____

20 _____ ● _____

_____

_____

_____

20 _____ ● _____

_____

_____

_____

20 _____ ● _____

_____

_____

_____

NOVEMBER 9

20 ___ •

20 ___ •

20 ___ •

20 ___ •

20 ___ •

NOVEMBER 10

20 ● _____

20 ● _____

20 ● _____

20 ● _____

20 ● _____

NOVEMBER 11

20 _____ • _____

_____

_____

_____

20 _____ • _____

_____

_____

_____

20 _____ • _____

_____

_____

_____

20 _____ • _____

_____

_____

_____

20 _____ • _____

_____

_____

_____

NOVEMBER 12

20 ● _____

20 ● _____

20 ● _____

20 ● _____

20 ● _____

NOVEMBER 13

20 ●

20 ●

20 ●

20 ●

20 ●

NOVEMBER 14

20   ● _____
_____
_____
_____

20   ● _____
_____
_____
_____

20   ● _____
_____
_____
_____

20   ● _____
_____
_____
_____

20   ● _____
_____
_____
_____

NOVEMBER 15

20 _____ ●

20 _____ ●

20 _____ ●

20 _____ ●

20 _____ ●

NOVEMBER 16

20 ●

20 ●

20 ●

20 ●

20 ●

NOVEMBER 17

20 _____ • _____

_____

_____

_____

20 _____ • _____

_____

_____

_____

20 _____ • _____

_____

_____

_____

20 _____ • _____

_____

_____

_____

20 _____ • _____

_____

_____

_____

NOVEMBER 18

20 ● _____

_____

_____

_____

20 ● _____

_____

_____

_____

20 ● _____

_____

_____

_____

20 ● _____

_____

_____

_____

20 ● _____

_____

_____

_____

NOVEMBER 19

20 ● _____

_____

_____

_____

20 ● _____

_____

_____

_____

20 ● _____

_____

_____

_____

20 ● _____

_____

_____

_____

20 ● _____

_____

_____

_____

NOVEMBER 20

20 _____ ● _____

_____

_____

_____

20 _____ ● _____

_____

_____

_____

20 _____ ● _____

_____

_____

_____

20 _____ ● _____

_____

_____

_____

20 _____ ● _____

_____

_____

_____

NOVEMBER 21

20 ● _____

_____

_____

_____

20 ● _____

_____

_____

_____

20 ● _____

_____

_____

_____

20 ● _____

_____

_____

_____

20 ● _____

_____

_____

_____

NOVEMBER 22

20   ●

20   ●

20   ●

20   ●

20   ●

NOVEMBER 23

20 _____ • _____

_____

_____

_____

20 _____ • _____

_____

_____

_____

20 _____ • _____

_____

_____

_____

20 _____ • _____

_____

_____

_____

20 _____ • _____

_____

_____

_____

NOVEMBER 24

20 •

20 •

20 •

20 •

20 •

NOVEMBER 25

20 ● _____

20 ● _____

20 ● _____

20 ● _____

20 ● _____

NOVEMBER 26

20 _____ • _____

_____

_____

_____

20 _____ • _____

_____

_____

_____

20 _____ • _____

_____

_____

_____

20 _____ • _____

_____

_____

_____

20 _____ • _____

_____

_____

_____

NOVEMBER 27

20 • _____

_____

_____

_____

20 • _____

_____

_____

_____

20 • _____

_____

_____

_____

20 • _____

_____

_____

_____

20 • _____

_____

_____

_____

NOVEMBER 28

20 ● _____

_____

_____

_____

20 ● _____

_____

_____

_____

20 ● _____

_____

_____

_____

20 ● _____

_____

_____

_____

20 ● _____

_____

_____

_____

NOVEMBER 29

20 ● _____

_____

_____

_____

20 ● _____

_____

_____

_____

20 ● _____

_____

_____

_____

20 ● _____

_____

_____

_____

20 ● _____

_____

_____

_____

NOVEMBER 30

20 ● _____

_____

_____

_____

20 ● _____

_____

_____

_____

20 ● _____

_____

_____

_____

20 ● _____

_____

_____

_____

20 ● _____

_____

_____

_____

DECEMBER 1

20 _____ • _____

_____

_____

_____

20 _____ • _____

_____

_____

_____

20 _____ • _____

_____

_____

_____

20 _____ • _____

_____

_____

_____

20 _____ • _____

_____

_____

_____

DECEMBER 2

20 ___ ● _____

_____

_____

_____

20 ___ ● _____

_____

_____

_____

20 ___ ● _____

_____

_____

_____

20 ___ ● _____

_____

_____

_____

20 ___ ● _____

_____

_____

_____

DECEMBER 3

20 _____ ● _____

_____

_____

_____

20 _____ ● _____

_____

_____

_____

20 _____ ● _____

_____

_____

_____

20 _____ ● _____

_____

_____

_____

20 _____ ● _____

_____

_____

_____

DECEMBER 4

20 ● _____

20 ● _____

20 ● _____

20 ● _____

20 ● _____

DECEMBER 5

20 ___ •

20 ___ •

20 ___ •

20 ___ •

20 ___ •

DECEMBER 6

20 ● _____

_____

_____

_____

20 ● _____

_____

_____

_____

20 ● _____

_____

_____

_____

20 ● _____

_____

_____

_____

20 ● _____

_____

_____

_____

DECEMBER 7

20 _____ • _____

_____

_____

_____

20 _____ • _____

_____

_____

_____

20 _____ • _____

_____

_____

_____

20 _____ • _____

_____

_____

_____

20 _____ • _____

_____

_____

_____

DECEMBER 8

20 _____ • _____

_____

_____

_____

20 _____ • _____

_____

_____

_____

20 _____ • _____

_____

_____

_____

20 _____ • _____

_____

_____

_____

20 _____ • _____

_____

_____

_____

DECEMBER 9

20 _____ • _____

_____

_____

_____

20 _____ • _____

_____

_____

_____

20 _____ • _____

_____

_____

_____

20 _____ • _____

_____

_____

_____

20 _____ • _____

_____

_____

_____

DECEMBER 10

20 _____ ● _____

_____

_____

_____

20 _____ ● _____

_____

_____

_____

20 _____ ● _____

_____

_____

_____

20 _____ ● _____

_____

_____

_____

20 _____ ● _____

_____

_____

_____

_____

DECEMBER 11

20 _____ ● _____

_____

_____

_____

20 _____ ● _____

_____

_____

_____

20 _____ ● _____

_____

_____

_____

20 _____ ● _____

_____

_____

_____

20 _____ ● _____

_____

_____

_____

DECEMBER 12

20 _____ • _____

_____

_____

_____

20 _____ • _____

_____

_____

_____

20 _____ • _____

_____

_____

_____

20 _____ • _____

_____

_____

_____

20 _____ • _____

_____

_____

_____

DECEMBER 13

20 _____ • _____

_____

_____

_____

20 _____ • _____

_____

_____

_____

20 _____ • _____

_____

_____

_____

20 _____ • _____

_____

_____

_____

20 _____ • _____

_____

_____

_____

DECEMBER 14

20 •
_____

20 •
_____

20 •
_____

20 •
_____

20 •
_____

DECEMBER 15

20 _____ ● _____

_____

_____

_____

20 _____ ● _____

_____

_____

_____

20 _____ ● _____

_____

_____

_____

20 _____ ● _____

_____

_____

_____

20 _____ ● _____

_____

_____

_____

DECEMBER 16

20 _____ • _____

_____

_____

_____

20 _____ • _____

_____

_____

_____

20 _____ • _____

_____

_____

_____

20 _____ • _____

_____

_____

_____

20 _____ • _____

_____

_____

_____

DECEMBER 17

20 ● _____

_____

_____

_____

20 ● _____

_____

_____

_____

20 ● _____

_____

_____

_____

20 ● _____

_____

_____

_____

20 ● _____

_____

_____

_____

DECEMBER 18

20 _____ • _____

_____

_____

_____

20 _____ • _____

_____

_____

_____

20 _____ • _____

_____

_____

_____

20 _____ • _____

_____

_____

_____

20 _____ • _____

_____

_____

_____

DECEMBER 19

20 _____ • _____

_____

_____

_____

20 _____ • _____

_____

_____

_____

20 _____ • _____

_____

_____

_____

20 _____ • _____

_____

_____

_____

20 _____ • _____

_____

_____

_____

DECEMBER 20

20 ____ ● _____

_____

_____

_____

20 ____ ● _____

_____

_____

_____

20 ____ ● _____

_____

_____

_____

20 ____ ● _____

_____

_____

_____

20 ____ ● _____

_____

_____

_____

DECEMBER 21

20 _____ • _____

_____

_____

_____

20 _____ • _____

_____

_____

_____

20 _____ • _____

_____

_____

_____

20 _____ • _____

_____

_____

_____

20 _____ • _____

_____

_____

_____

DECEMBER 22

20 ● _____

_____

_____

_____

20 ● _____

_____

_____

_____

20 ● _____

_____

_____

_____

20 ● _____

_____

_____

_____

20 ● _____

_____

_____

_____

DECEMBER 23

20 ____ • _____

_____

_____

_____

20 ____ • _____

_____

_____

_____

20 ____ • _____

_____

_____

_____

20 ____ • _____

_____

_____

_____

20 ____ • _____

_____

_____

_____

DECEMBER 24

20 •

20 •

20 •

20 •

20 •

DECEMBER 25

20 ● _____
_____
_____
_____

20 ● _____
_____
_____
_____

20 ● _____
_____
_____
_____

20 ● _____
_____
_____
_____

20 ● _____
_____
_____
_____

DECEMBER 26

20 _____ • _____

_____

_____

_____

20 _____ • _____

_____

_____

_____

20 _____ • _____

_____

_____

_____

20 _____ • _____

_____

_____

_____

20 _____ • _____

_____

_____

_____

DECEMBER 27

20 _____ • _____

_____

_____

_____

20 _____ • _____

_____

_____

_____

20 _____ • _____

_____

_____

_____

20 _____ • _____

_____

_____

_____

20 _____ • _____

_____

_____

_____

DECEMBER 28

20 ● _____

_____

_____

_____

20 ● _____

_____

_____

_____

20 ● _____

_____

_____

_____

20 ● _____

_____

_____

_____

20 ● _____

_____

_____

_____

DECEMBER 29

20 _____ • _____

_____

_____

_____

20 _____ • _____

_____

_____

_____

20 _____ • _____

_____

_____

_____

20 _____ • _____

_____

_____

_____

20 _____ • _____

_____

_____

_____

DECEMBER 30

20 ● _____
_____
_____
_____

20 ● _____
_____
_____
_____

20 ● _____
_____
_____
_____

20 ● _____
_____
_____
_____

20 ● _____
_____
_____
_____

DECEMBER 31

20____ •_____

_____

_____

_____

20____ •_____

_____

_____

_____

20____ •_____

_____

_____

_____

20____ •_____

_____

_____

_____

20____ •_____

_____

_____

_____

DATES TO REMEMBER

DATES TO REMEMBER